Lexi Catt's Meowmoirs—Tales of Heroic Scientists

LEXI AND LISTER

Keen, Marian, 1935-, author
    Lexi and Lister : defeat death / Marian Keen ; illustrated by
Jodie Dias, Wendy Watson.

(Lexi Catt's meowmoirs--tales of heroic scientists)
Issued in print and electronic formats.
ISBN 978-1-77141-097-7 (pbk.).--ISBN 978-1-77141-098-4 (html)

    I. Dias, Jodie, 1968-, illustrator II. Watson, Wendy, 1960-,
illustrator III. Title.

PS8621.E355L493 2015   jC813'.6   C2014-907753-X

                                        C2014-907754-8

Lexi Catt's Meowmoirs—Tales of Heroic Scientists

LEXI AND LISTER
Defeat Death

By Marian Keen

Illustrated by Jodie Dias and Wendy Watson
Edited by Nancy Wickham

First Published in Canada 2015 by Life Journey Publishing

Editor: Nina Shoroplova
Assistant Editor: Susan Kehoe
Production Editor: Jennifer Kaleta
Story Development Editor: Jodie Dias
Development Editor: Nancy Wickham
Illustrators: Jodie Dias, Wendy Watson
Cover Illustration: Jodie Dias, Wendy Watson
Book Cover Design: Marla Thompson
Typeset: Greg Salisbury
Photographer: Wendy Watson

Dedicated to
Curious and courageous scientists—past, present, and future—who pursue their new ideas, even amid resistance from colleagues.

The future will belong not to the conquerors,
but to those who have done the most for suffering humanity.
~ Louis Pasteur

TESTIMONIALS

"Marian Keen creates an appealing way for middle-grade students to learn about important historical figures. Readers will feel like they are dropped in to the surgical world, experiencing the frustrations and triumphs with Dr. Lister, as he makes important leaps in the medical field. Keen writes in a simple yet engaging manner that allows children to read with ease and access history through literature."

**Amanda Chura, Teacher Librarian,
Diefenbaker Elementary School**

"What captures me in each of Marian's stories in the Lexi collection is how playful they are, while holding onto accurate details. The books are clearly well-researched, and they teach so much. The stories bring the history to life in a way that children can connect to, sparking their curiosity and natural sense for fun."

**Laura Pearson, Teacher Librarian,
École Elémentaire William Bridge Elementary School**

ACKNOWLEDGEMENTS

I wish to express profound and sincere appreciation to John Dias, my son-in-law, for the inspiration and concept of the *Lexi Catt Series*, which brings to life the history of medicine. Alexander Catt II, also known as Lexi, is a wonderful spokes-feline, who has allowed me to share my interest in the health sciences with children. Thank you, John, for opening the door to these exciting adventures.

I wish to thank Julie Salisbury and her team at Influence Publishing for the opportunity to bring Lexi's eye on history to publication. Children now have the chance to become acquainted with some true heroes of history.

I wish to thank my daughters, Jodie Dias and Wendy Watson, for bringing the story to life with charming, whimsical visuals, while maintaining the historical truth.

I wish to thank Nancy Wickham for her meticulous attention to detail and clarity in editing my written words and her patience in dealing with my cockeyed humour.

I want my family to know that I appreciate their patience and support in this endeavour by never complaining about the long hours I spend on this project.

TABLE OF CONTENTS

LIST OF ILLUSTRATIONS

Lexi Catt

Map of Western Europe

Our new family

Lexi Catt

LEXI CATT'S MEOWMOIRS

My name is Alexander Catt II, but people call me Lexi. I was born in Luxor, Egypt, during Ramses' reign as pharaoh. My father was Alexander Catt, the adventurer, and my mother was called Ebony. I am all black like my mother, but I have a white muzzle, white paws, and a small tip of white on my talented tail. I have already lived eight of my nine lives and my *purr*pose now is to write the *tails* of my adventures in my *meow*moirs like my father wrote his before me.

Pssst!

A memoir is an historical account
written from personal knowledge.
Lexi calls his memoirs,
"meowmoirs."

I have a peculiar attraction to trouble. Fortunately, the strange twitch of my tail warns me when trouble is near. For this reason, I have always tried to live with scientists or doctors of medicine over the centuries. You never know when you'll need a doctor in the house!

In this *tail* of adventure, I live with a famous doctor of medicine, Joseph Lister, the Father of Modern Surgery. I will tell you how Joseph defeats death through handwashing and sterilizing surgical equipment, preventing the spread of life-threatening infections.

Map of Western Europe

Our new family

Chapter One

An Unusual Honeymoon

"Mee—ouch!" I protested.

"Hold sssstill!" Mama hissed.

Mama was giving me a bath. Bath time always took too long, and interrupted playtime, but today, Mama was much too vigorous and particularly fussy about the procedure. Not only was she especially fussy, she was also teaching me each and every rule about the task.

I thought I knew all the rules about baths, so it was irritating to hear it all again as her rough tongue demonstrated every point of her lecture.

At last, Mama sat back on her haunches and said, "That is the last time I'm giving you your bath. From now on you will do it for yourself, so remember all I taught you and keep yourself clean!"

"Why, Mama?" I asked.

"Because you are going to live with a new doctor."

"A new doctor? Mama?"

"Yes. Dr. Joseph Lister. Agnes is going to marry Dr. Joe and you are going to be Agnes's cat!"

"I love Agnes! She's pretty, she's gentle, and she's smart!" I mewed.

"Then listen to her and be a good cat. Stay out of trouble!" said Mama.

Mama's words echoed in my head as Doctor Symes, Agnes's father, came into the kitchen and scooped me up.

"Thank you, Ebony, for preparing Lexi. I'm sure Agnes will be happy to have such a smart and well-mannered feline."

And with that, the good doctor whisked me into the parlour where he presented me as a gift to Agnes and Joe.

"Your mother and I want you to have a little something from home," he said. "You have always loved your mother's cat, Ebony. This is her son, Lexi, for your new home."

Agnes cuddled me. "Oh! Thank you, Father!" Sitting beside her, her fiancé, Doctor Joseph Lister, gave me a gentle pat, too.

"He is a handsome fellow," he pronounced. Right away I knew that Joseph was smart.

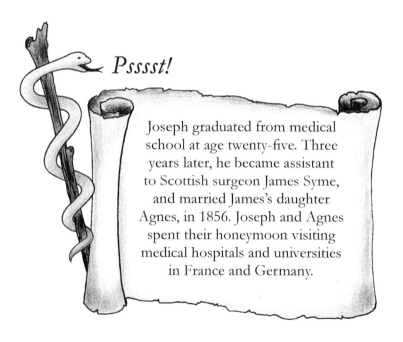

Psssst!

Joseph graduated from medical school at age twenty-five. Three years later, he became assistant to Scottish surgeon James Syme, and married James's daughter Agnes, in 1856. Joseph and Agnes spent their honeymoon visiting medical hospitals and universities in France and Germany.

Dirty paws—Me-eww!

A few days later, Joe and Agnes were wed, and the three of us went on our honeymoon to Europe. I travelled in Agnes's carpetbag.

The train and coach rides were so smooth, they rocked me to sleep. But the boat ride upset my tummy. *Mew!* Agnes's tummy was upset, too. It was lucky for us to have a doctor along, for Dr. Joe knew just the thing to settle our tummies.

Once again on dry land, however, the upset tummy experience was bliss compared to the near dying of boredom from the medical tours. *Meow!* The good doctor took us to tour universities and hospitals, and then hospitals and universities. Once or twice, Agnes suggested a concert or a museum, but then she became so interested in medical issues that she began to take notes. *Yawn!* I slept at her feet.

We even watched an operation. Doctor Joe shook hands with the surgeon, who at least wiped his bloody hands first. I kept my paws to myself. *Me-eww!*

After we left, Agnes said, "Their coats get so dirty, Joseph. Promise me, dear, that you will keep clean!"

Dr. Joe laughed. "We have to expect that, Agnes; it is part of the operating scene."

At last, we returned home to Glasgow, a city in Scotland, where Dr. Joe was an assistant surgeon and lecturer. *Meow!* He was a smart fellow!

Agnes was busy setting up our new household. As she unpacked the wedding presents, I inspected every one. I padded around the crystal and china with such great delicacy that Agnes smiled.

Every evening she turned up the gaslight and read *The Lancet* and other medical books and papers to Dr. Joe while he rested his eyes. He explained terms, and they discussed medical problems for hours. As I lay purring by the fire, I would listen intently to many of the medical stories.

One journal explained the theories of Dr. Semmelweis of Vienna, Austria who was certain that doctors were transmitting bad fevers. The doctors were angry and so insulted that they labelled him a troublemaker.

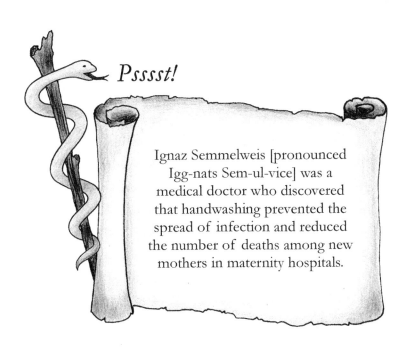

Psssst!

Ignaz Semmelweis [pronounced Igg-nats Sem-ul-vice] was a medical doctor who discovered that handwashing prevented the spread of infection and reduced the number of deaths among new mothers in maternity hospitals.

I inspected every present.

Agnes said, "Poor man."

Dr. Joe said, "No doctor likes to be told they are responsible for illness. We consider it our duty to save lives. We are doing our best, and Semmelweis is discrediting our work. Semmelweis should make his point in a more diplomatic way. Calling the doctors 'murderers' is insulting. He should prove his point with careful experiments."

Dr. Joe set up his own laboratory in the hospital and, with Agnes's help, he started to conduct these experiments himself. Agnes took me everywhere she went, so of course she brought me to the lab, and I inspected the vials and bowls as carefully as I had inspected the wedding gifts, and she smiled at me again.

Sounds very peaceful and orderly, doesn't it? *Meow!* It didn't last long enough. Our peace was destroyed by a mewling, puking "gift."

Baby Bart mewed a lot.

Chapter Two

A Honey of a Mess!

One day, Agnes was in the lab, busy writing up notes on Dr. Joe's latest experiment. Curled up on her lap, I was trying to stay still so I wouldn't disturb her, but my tail began to twitch, and I couldn't sleep. And I knew that my tail twitching meant trouble was just around the corner.

"Lexi! For goodness sake, if you can't stay still, go sit on the windowsill. You're distracting me from my work," said Agnes.

At that moment, Dr. Joe came into the lab.

"Time to take a rest, my dear," he said. "You have been working all morning and I have a surprise for you."

"A surprise?" asked Agnes.

"Yes. Though, it is rather sad. A lady died on the ward today, and she left an orphan … this little fellow!" said Dr. Joe as he brought out of his pocket a small and fluffy, grey ball of fur.

Once out of his warm pocket, the little kitten began to mew … and mew … and mew!

One look and I knew we were in for trouble. The kitten was almost newborn, and so dirty it was difficult to tell what colour he really was. And the mewing!

"The poor creature! He is hungry!" said Agnes. "I will need

some milk and towels and a basin of warm water. The kitchen!" She hurried off with the kitten.

"Well, Lexi, I guess we are left on our own," observed Dr. Joe. "I have work to do. Keep an eye on that bit of fluff; he has not had the benefit of a mother cat to teach him the facts of life."

And with that piece of advice, Dr. Joe marched back to his hospital ward where patients had dire troubles of their own.

Dr. Joe's words weighed down my whiskers with responsibility. I wondered, how much trouble could a tiny kitten be? So, being the curious cat that I am, I padded off to the hospital's kitchen. Agnes had cleaned up the mewing white ball and wrapped him in a warm towel. Squirming inside the towel on a shelf of the big iron stove, the kitten was still mewing. Agnes was heating some milk. She tied a knot in her handkerchief and dipped a small corner into the milk and offered it to the kitten. He seemed irritated by the handkerchief and mewed even louder—if that was possible—and turned his head away. Agnes was patient, but after several tries, she forced his mouth open and pushed in the handkerchief. At last, the mewing stopped as he sucked on the linen.

Dorie, one of the kitchen helpers, watched and asked, "What are you going to call 'im, Ma'am?"

"'Bartholo*mew*,' because because he mews a lot," laughed Agnes.

"He surely does, Ma'am!" laughed Dorie. "But that's a big name for such a tiny critter."

"He will grow; look at him eat. But until he has grown to fit his name, I shall call him 'Bart' for short."

A honey of a mess!

"Meow," I thought. "The middle letters in his name should be reversed. His name should be 'BRAT,' not 'Bart'!"

We took him home that night, but Agnes didn't get much sleep. For many nights, the mewing "Brat" fussed and sucked on the handkerchief soaked in milk. But at last, he slept for some of the night, and became more active during the day. One day, he frolicked around the kitchen floor while I lapped my milk.

"This is how a real cat drinks milk," I said to him. After all, he had no mother and he needed someone to teach him. I continued to lap.

The little Brat put his paw into my bowl and pulled. The milk spilled onto the floor. He scampered off.

"Lexi!" scolded the kitchen maid, Annie. "You've spilled your milk, you naughty cat!"

Agnes looked up and I slunk away. She shook her head. I don't know if she thought I'd really spilled my milk or not. Agnes knew I wasn't a clumsy feline.

Some weeks later, the Brat showed his true nature. Annie had set the breakfast table and left to get some linen napkins. The cook was busy at the stove. Here was his chance. He had grown quite leggy and began to leap about exploring. He leaped up to a chair and then to the table.

My tail was twitching and that twitch always told me trouble was about to happen. I escaped into the pantry and watched. No way did I want to get blamed for what he might do next.

He prowled around the breakfast table and settled on the messiest item he could find—the honey pot. I saw at once that this was no clumsy cat. He deliberately pushed the pot over onto the crisp, clean tablecloth, and carefully walked through the spreading puddle of amber waves of sticky bee juice. He tasted it and dipped his muzzle into it. Then he rolled in it!

Returning with the linen napkins, Annie shrieked, "You naughty kitten! What a mess! Now I have to fetch a new table-cloth!" She wrapped the Brat in a napkin so she could lift him, and then threw him into the pantry and slammed the door. Now, the naughty kitty was my problem.

I set to work at once. Holding the squirming Brat with one paw, I gave his creamy coat of fur a thorough bath. The worst part was listening to his constant mewing. But I also heard through the door that we had a guest join us for breakfast and so, as soon as I could, I meowed to be let out of the pantry. Agnes let us out and picked up the Brat before he could do any more harm.

They had finished breakfast, and Dr. Joe fed me table scraps of bacon and fish, while he chatted with his guest, Thomas Anderson, the chemist.

Chuckling over Bart's mischief, Dr. Joe said, "I see he has been cleaned up. Lexi must have given him a bath. What a sticky fur ball that would be!"

I guess they thought it was a big joke, but I was sure thirsty! *Meow!*

Mr. Anderson excused himself. "I must return to my lab. I say, I think you will be very interested in Mr. Pasteur's information. It really explains the mystery of microbes. Those tiny organisms can cause grape juice to turn into wine as it ferments. And, they can cause milk to spoil and meat to rot.

Hold still, Brat; you need a bath!

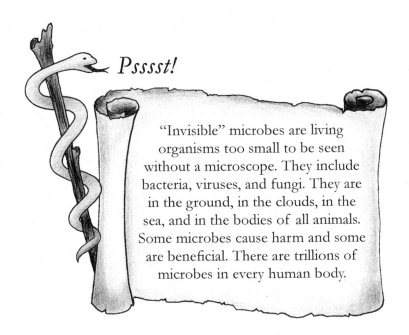

Psssst!

"Invisible" microbes are living organisms too small to be seen without a microscope. They include bacteria, viruses, and fungi. They are in the ground, in the clouds, in the sea, and in the bodies of all animals. Some microbes cause harm and some are beneficial. There are trillions of microbes in every human body.

It's amazing!

"Now Pasteur can control those microbes. He also confirms Dr. Semmelweis's observations about the importance of handwashing. Pasteur's information should be helpful to you as you work to prevent infections, Joseph."

Mr. Anderson continued. "You will see it is not the AIR, itself; it is something IN the air. The rest of the doctors would rather blame miasma, 'bad air.' They think there is nothing they can do about it, but Mr. Pasteur shows that this is not true. Anyway, good luck with it.

"Thank you, kind Agnes, for a nourishing breakfast. It gives me a good start to the day."

"I will see you to the door," said Dr. Joe. "And thank you! I am deeply grateful for the information, Thomas."

My favourite time of day

CHAPTER THREE

CRYSTALS TO THE RESCUE

That night, Agnes turned up the kerosene lamp and read Louis Pasteur's paper from the *Chemistry Journal*. Dr. Joe lay back on the sofa with his eyes closed. But he was far from asleep. His arm dangled down, and he scratched my ears gently as he listened. I purred in pleasure, but I listened, too.

When Agnes finished reading, she asked, "What do you think, dear?"

Dr. Joe responded, "I am thinking of all those unfortunate people who have died of sepsis or who have lost their arms or legs because of infections, while the medical world has shrugged and said, 'It's miasma! We can do nothing about it!'

"Now, because my father improved the microscope, Pasteur has found it possible to see clearly into the invisible world. With this microscope, Pasteur observes that it is not the air itself, but rather living creatures—'microbes'—in the air that cause the rotting, stinking infections that we doctors have fought so hard to defeat."

Agnes added, "It has taken the work of many men to find these answers."

"Yes," said Dr. Joe. "Dr. Semmelweis showed us with his statistics that infections are contagious. My father made it possible for us to see microbes with his improved microscope. And Louis Pasteur has proven that microbes cause infections. He also tells us what to do to stop infections: filter the microbes, or kill them with heat or chemicals."

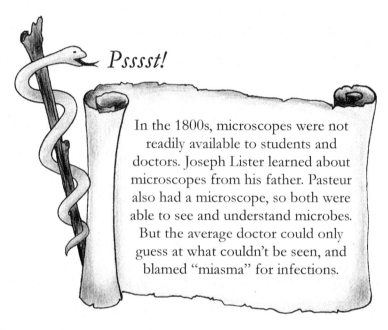

Psssst!

In the 1800s, microscopes were not readily available to students and doctors. Joseph Lister learned about microscopes from his father. Pasteur also had a microscope, so both were able to see and understand microbes. But the average doctor could only guess at what couldn't be seen, and blamed "miasma" for infections.

Agnes said, "Now, it is up to you, Joseph. You must find a way to defeat death from these microbes. What do you think you might try?"

"Well, my dear," Dr. Joe considered, "one cannot filter a body, and by cutting the infection out, the patient loses a part of their body. We cannot burn the body. So that leaves chemical treatment as the best possibility.

"Perhaps we should invite Mr. Pasteur to come and join us here in Scotland. I'd like to discuss it with him, but I can't wait for that. So meanwhile, I'll ask our own chemist for help. First thing tomorrow morning, I shall ask Thomas Anderson to help me find a chemical to kill these microbes before they kill us. Usually our skin protects us from these tiny microbes. That is our natural filter. But when the skin is broken by an injury or an operation, that is when we need a chemical.

"Thomas will know what to do."

The next day Agnes and I went to the lab as usual. Unfortunately, the Brat came too. I sat on my usual perch on the windowsill. From there I could see and hear everything in the room and not be blamed for any trouble that the Brat might cause.

Dr. Joe burst into the room carrying a large jar of white crystals. "Agnes! This may be the answer to the gangrene infections that are killing patients!" he shouted in his excitement.

"What is it?" asked Agnes.

"Carbolic acid in crystal form!" Dr. Joe explained excitedly.

"Where did you get it?"

"From Thomas," answered Dr. Joe. "Thomas said that creosote is used to keep railroad ties and wooden ships from rotting. Creosote is made from coal tar, and so is carbolic acid. Thomas told me another chemist named Lamaire said that carbolic acid is used to keep sewers from smelling of rotten waste. He also said carbolic acid is curing cattle of parasites, so he is suggesting that carbolic acid could keep a wound from rotting. We must try it, Agnes!

"Now, where is that frog we were working on?"

Another doctor walked in.

"What is all the excitement, Joseph? I could hear you from the hall."

Dr. Joe grinned. "We are about to stop gangrene before it kills this frog."

The other doctor looked at the frog.

The frog test did not go well.

"It has pus on its leg. Good. That means the wound is healing. It has to go through that stage before it gets better."

"I do not agree; but we will soon see," said Dr. Joe who was busy dissolving crystals in a little jar of water. He dabbed the solution onto the frog's leg. From the look on Dr. Joe's face, I thought the dabbing hadn't gone well.

The visiting doctor shrugged. "Now you have burned the leg. I told you it would not work."

He walked out.

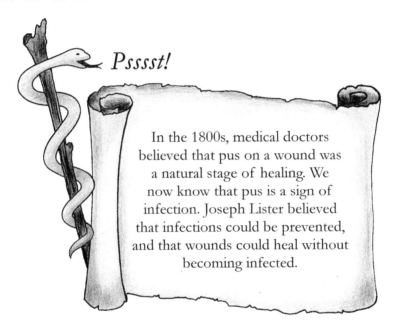

Psssst!

In the 1800s, medical doctors believed that pus on a wound was a natural stage of healing. We now know that pus is a sign of infection. Joseph Lister believed that infections could be prevented, and that wounds could heal without becoming infected.

Dr. Joe and Agnes tried several liquids and diluted them so they wouldn't burn. Paraffin oil and carbolic acid made a paste, which they thought might work better, because it would stick to the wound.

Hours passed and there were many jars spread out on the table. The room smelled rather sickly sweet. My tail twitched! The next moment, Bart the Brat decided to help! O-*Meow!*

Cat and cart collide with a crash!

Chapter Four

A Feline Operation

It happened so fast I'm not sure how it did. Bart somehow used a chair and the rolling service cart to get up to the lab table.

Agnes said, "Bart! Off the table!"

But the Brat had already reached his target—the big jar of carbolic acid crystals. Rearing up onto his hind feet, he tried to smell it or taste it or tip it. I don't know which he intended to do.

Dr. Joe tried to grab the bratty mischief-maker, but the cart was in his way. He crashed into it making it roll across the room, hit the wall, and bounce back.

At the same time, Agnes reached for the jar and held on to it.

Bart tried to evade both of them and leaped from the table right into the path of the rolling cart.

"Yow-screeech!" screamed Bart and he fell like a stuffy onto the hard floor. He didn't move.

Agnes went to pick him up, but Dr. Joe stopped her. He knelt down and looked closely at Bart. The Brat was breathing, but a trickle of blood stained his front leg.

"Is he dead?" asked Agnes, white with fear.

"No, but he has a compound fracture," replied Dr. Joe quietly.

"Oh, Joseph, do you think you will have to take his leg off?"
Dr. Joe looked at the jar of carbolic acid.

"Maybe not, dear. Let's see if these crystals can do what they say they can do. Let's operate and set the kitten's leg."

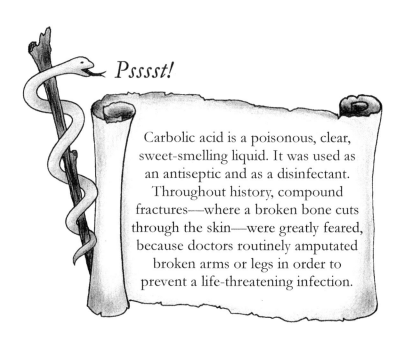

Psssst!

Carbolic acid is a poisonous, clear, sweet-smelling liquid. It was used as an antiseptic and as a disinfectant. Throughout history, compound fractures—where a broken bone cuts through the skin—were greatly feared, because doctors routinely amputated broken arms or legs in order to prevent a life-threatening infection.

They set to work. They cleared the table and gathered gauze, towels, and bowls of the new solution. They washed their own hands in the carbolic acid solution and gently moved Bart onto the table. Dr. Joe set to work. All this activity was done very quietly. Dr. Joe and Agnes had worked together for so long that she didn't need directions, and he relied on her. It was almost too quiet.

I missed Bart's mewing.

I hopped down from the windowsill and up onto the table silently. They paid no attention to me. I watched Bart. He was still breathing, but he was asleep. Then I knew why it was so quiet. Bart wasn't mewing, and I missed him.

Dr. Joe set the kitten's leg and poured the carbolic acid solution over it.

He soaked the gauze in the solution and wrapped the open wound. Then, he fastened splints onto the leg and taped the whole thing together.

"Now comes the hard part, Agnes," he sighed. "We have to keep him quiet for a few days. He must not move his leg."

"Leave it to Lexi and me. I'll wrap him like a mummy so he cannot move. Let's put a bit of laudanum in his milk; I can feed him with my handkerchief," said Agnes. "And Lexi can help me keep watch."

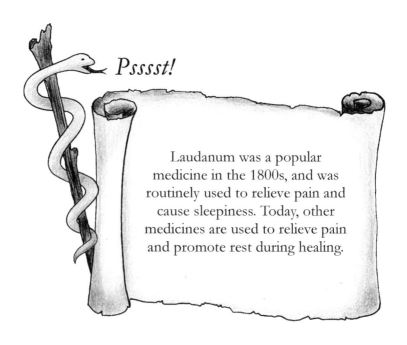

Psssst!

Laudanum was a popular medicine in the 1800s, and was routinely used to relieve pain and cause sleepiness. Today, other medicines are used to relieve pain and promote rest during healing.

The rest of the day passed slowly. Agnes and I watched over Bart and, although he opened his eyes, he didn't even twitch. Dr. Joe brought Agnes pillows and a blanket, and she sat in the chair and dozed off a few times during the night.

The following morning, Bart opened his eyes. His whiskers twitched. Agnes was asleep, so I meowed loudly. She woke up and soothed him and fed him more milk. She offered me some too, but I didn't want any sleeping powder.

Dr. Joe came in and sent Agnes home to rest and eat, and I went home with her. The days passed like that until the fourth day.

"Little Bart looks more alert today," said Dr. Joe. "Let's have a look at his leg." Carefully, he unwrapped the bandaging. There was a scab over the wound, but there was no pus.

"No infection!" exclaimed Dr. Joe and Agnes together, and they grinned.

"But he still has to keep his leg immobile until the bone sets and that may take six weeks," cautioned Dr. Joe.

He soaked more bandages in the solution and wrapped up Bart's leg with the splints.

Soon the hospital nurses heard about Bart, and Agnes had plenty of help keeping him quiet, fed, and happy. In fact, he had so much attention, he didn't even mew.

No doctors came in to see the "miracle kitten" as the nurses called him. I think the doctors were jealous of Dr. Joe's success.

After many weeks confined to hospital care, Bart was taken home for Annie to look after him. She placed him at his bowl of food, which he ate with gusto until he tired. He then dragged his splinted leg back to his basket. Annie lifted him into his basket where he slept like a baby.

At last, the six weeks was up, and Dr. Joe took Bart back to the lab to remove the splints and bandages. He stood Bart on his feet. Bart swayed a bit and looked over the edge of the table. Then he sat. Never again did Bart ever leap up onto a table. Bowls, vases, jars, and honey pots were once again safe. Bart had become a floor cat.

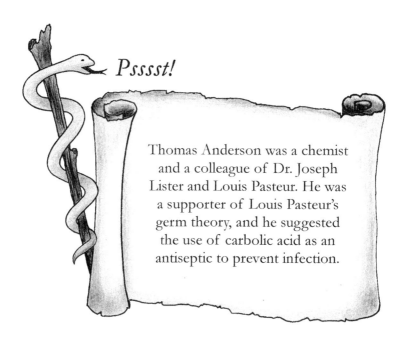

Pssst!

Thomas Anderson was a chemist and a colleague of Dr. Joseph Lister and Louis Pasteur. He was a supporter of Louis Pasteur's germ theory, and he suggested the use of carbolic acid as an antiseptic to prevent infection.

Dr. Joe tried to tell the other doctors about Pasteur's microbes and the treatment with carbolic acid, but they scoffed.

"Have you ever seen a microbe?" one doctor asked another.

"Not I!" he replied. "They are invisible you know!" and he laughed.

Dr. Joe explained, "You have to look through a microscope!"

A third doctor mewed. "I'm a busy man. I haven't hours to waste in a lab looking for invisible microbes."

Agnes wrung her hands. "They are so stubborn it is exasperating! Why will they not listen?"

Dr. Joe said, "The medical schools will not provide microscopes for their students. So, they do not even know how to use them. Be patient, Agnes. Soon we will have an opportunity to prove it to them. Meanwhile, I shall perfect our method."

Then, one day, with a lot of noise, opportunity entered the hospital.

Saving a limb and a life

Chapter Five

Another Antiseptic Operation

Once again, Dr. Joe, Agnes, and I were in the lab. My tail began to twitch … and twitch … and twitch. It was twitching so much, I began to pace.

A woman began to shriek loudly in the admitting room, "No! No! No!"

Naturally, we rushed to see what the matter was. A boy lay on the examination table. He held his bleeding leg with both hands. A bone stuck out. Even I knew it was the dreaded compound fracture.

A doctor kindly put a hand on the woman's shoulder. "I know it is hard, Mrs. Greenlees, but we must take the leg or he will die of gangrene."

"Mother! Please! Do not let them! I would rather die than give up running!" pleaded her son.

His mother's face was covered in tears. "Please. There must be something you can do. At least TRY to save Jimmy's leg. Please."

She turned when she saw Dr. Joe. "Can you help me? They want to take his leg off. He's only eleven years old, and he loves to run."

Dr. Joe looked at the other two doctors. One explained, "He

was run over by a runaway wagon. The break is very bad. If we do not amputate his leg, he will die of gangrene."

The other doctor smirked, "Unless you want to perform 'cat surgery' on him."

"Cat surgery?" asked the boy's mother.

"I have set a compound fracture, without gangrene, on a young cat," said Dr. Joe. "I expect I could do the same for a young boy, but I cannot guarantee it."

The boy's mother looked at her son, who had passed out. "Would you please try, Doctor?"

Dr. Joe ordered preparations. The other two doctors left, shaking their heads.

Dr. Joe didn't trust that the operating room was clean enough, so he ordered that it be washed well with carbolic acid solution. Agnes gave him an empty perfume atomizer, which he filled with the solution to spray the room during the operation. Then, he washed his hands and the instruments in the solution as well. Finally, he cleaned the wound with the carbolic solution and began to set the bone.

Thomas Anderson, Agnes, and I watched the procedure. But there were no other doctors present, because they had too little curiosity, too much envy, and no trust in a new idea.

Dr. Joe did everything he could to ensure that the operation was infection-free, just as he had done with Bart. Finally, he covered the bandage with a strong fabric.

"There! That will protect the wound from the nasty microbes. Now, we wait!" he said.

At least, the nurses were helpful. They had helped with Bart's recovery and knew that young James had to be kept quiet.

Four days is a long time to wait.

At last, Dr. Joe said, "Let's take a look at his leg."

We all gathered around Jimmy's bed to see the result. Agnes, Jimmy's mother, Thomas, and I held our breath as the last sticky bandage was carefully lifted.

There, at last, we saw that a scab had grown over the wound. No pus. No infection. No gangrene. Dr. Joe looked at Jimmy and smiled. Jimmy grinned back. He knew his leg was saved. Dr. Joe carefully explained that it would be difficult to keep his leg still for six weeks, but he must not risk further injury. Jimmy solemnly promised to do his best.

Psssst!

In August 1865, eleven–year-old Jimmy Greenlees was brought to the Glasgow hospital with a compound fracture of his leg: the wheel of a cart had run over him. Dr. Joseph Lister applied a carbolic acid solution to prevent infection, set the leg, and the boy's leg healed without infection.

Jimmy walks away; Bart goes too.

Six weeks is a lot longer than four days. To lie still that long could make anyone depressed. I could see it was tough on Jimmy who was an active boy by nature. His mother read to him and the nurses gave him as much attention as they could.

To cheer Jimmy up, Agnes brought Bart in for a visit. Once placed on the bed, the Brat stayed there, because he was afraid to jump off the high bed. Jimmy petted the kitten until they both fell asleep. After that, Agnes brought Bart every afternoon for a visit.

The six weeks passed slowly, but at last the day arrived when Jimmy walked out of the hospital on his own two legs. He had become very fond of Bart and Bart followed him out of the hospital. With tears in her eyes, Agnes let her kitten go to his new home, with Jimmy.

I thought, "Finally, the Brat has lived up to his long name, 'Bartholomew.'" I would miss him in a way, but I was rather relieved to be the only cat in the Lister home once more.

News of success for The Lancet

Chapter Six

The Queen Trusts Dr. Joe

There was no celebration at the hospital. No doctors congratulated Dr. Joe. No doctor even asked how Dr. Joe had done it. They probably thought he was just lucky. But Dr. Joe continued his research tirelessly.

Then, one day, a doctor begrudgingly came into the lab and asked, "Do you want to set another leg?"

Dr. Joe eagerly took every opportunity to save a leg or arm from amputation following a compound fracture. Agnes wrote up every case.

"They want me to do all the compound fractures," said Dr. Joe, "but they do not even notice that I am using this antiseptic method with other operations without the usual infections. How can I convince them to try this, too?" he asked Agnes.

She said, "Remember Dr. Semmelweis? He did not use the microscope. He did not do experiments to prove his theories. By the time he published, every doctor was already mad at him."

"But he was right," said Dr. Joe.

"Others have been right, too, but that is not enough," said Agnes. "To get people to understand, you have to prove what you know is true, and, Joseph, you have to publish what you know in an accepted journal like *The Lancet.* People believe what they see in print."

Psssst!

Including Jimmy Greenlees, four of Lister's early successes treating compound fractures with carbolic acid were children aged between five and eleven. Lister was well-known for his sympathetic nature and kindness, especially with his younger patients.

"How long has it been since we set Jimmy's leg?"

"Almost two years."

"How many compound fractures have we set?"

"Eleven."

"That is enough to start. Let's write them up from your notes, Agnes."

They set to work assembling the notes from the eleven cases. Working every night they wrote, rewrote, edited, and polished until the article was ready for publication.

The article was entitled, "Antiseptic Principles of the Practice of Surgery," and was published in *The Lancet* on September 21, 1867.

The doctors at the Glasgow hospital gradually accepted Dr. Joe's methods of antiseptic surgery. They even removed their frock coats and put on aprons over their waistcoats. The number of infections went way down. Many lives were saved. Agnes and I were so proud.

Pssst!

Lister wrote a series of articles for *The Lancet*, sharing his work on preventing infection. It has been said that these articles have saved more lives than any other articles ever published.

Dr. Joe continued to improve the procedures. He paid attention to the equipment and materials used in operations. He advised that the instruments used in surgery should have handles that were not porous, so that germs couldn't take refuge in them.

He also noted that doctors reused the linen and silk threads used to sew up wounds. Doctors called these threads "ligatures," and they stored them, still bloody, in their coat buttonholes! He insisted the threads should be soaked in carbolic acid. He used sterilized silver wire to join broken bones.

Dr. Joe saved even more lives by soaking the rubber tubing used to drain pus from big blisters, called abscesses, in carbolic acid.

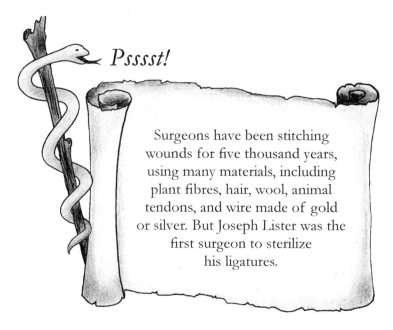

Pssst!

Surgeons have been stitching wounds for five thousand years, using many materials, including plant fibres, hair, wool, animal tendons, and wire made of gold or silver. But Joseph Lister was the first surgeon to sterilize his ligatures.

Then one day, a carriage came to the back door of the hospital. A small lady entered, dressed all in black with heavy veils over her face. She nearly stepped on me, but I moved aside and tucked in my tail. She saw me then, and gave me a proper pat on my head. My whiskers! It was Queen Victoria herself! *Meow!*

Dr. Joe had an operating room all cleaned and ready for her. His new carbolic acid misting machine was automatically spraying the room.

From the lab across the hall, I watched the Queen enter the operating room.

"Dr. Lister, how can you work in this mist?" she asked.

"We do not like it! Shut it off!"

Dr. Joe said, "It is a necessary evil incurred to attain a greater good."

"Dr. Lister, your skin is bleached and your nails are cracked."

"My lungs are sore, too."

"We do not like it then," said the Queen. "So, shut it off!"

Dr. Joe did shut off his misting machine and then proceeded to drain an abscess from the Queen's arm with the antiseptic rubber tubing. He cleaned and bandaged the wound. The Queen remained well and lived a long life.

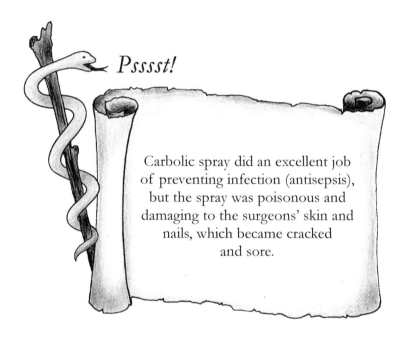

Pssst!

Carbolic spray did an excellent job of preventing infection (antisepsis), but the spray was poisonous and damaging to the surgeons' skin and nails, which became cracked and sore.

One day soon after the Queen's operation, a doctor came to see Dr. Joe in his lab. "Lister, I've just returned from London. I had the opportunity to watch many operations there."

"London is a great learning centre; they must be accomplishing great things," said Dr. Joe.

"In truth, they're not doing as well as we are. The incidence of infections is much higher. But worse ..." he paused.

Dr. Joe put down his vial, "Worse?"

"You have become the target of a standing joke there."

"Oh? What have I done that is so funny?"

"Nothing, of course, but every time someone enters the operating room, they shout, 'Close the door! You will let in Lister's microbes!' They yelled at me more than once, and they seem to find it a great joke."

"Somebody should explain it to them," said Dr. Joe calmly.

"Yes! You! That is why I took the liberty of nominating you for an appointment to the King's College Hospital in London. I hope you do not mind. I am sure Agnes would be in favour of your teaching those rascals a lesson!"

They're invisible!

CHAPTER SEVEN

DR. JOE AND THE HEAD CAT

"Move?" Agnes asked in surprise.

"Yes," said Dr. Joe, quietly.

"To London?" Agnes sounded doubtful.

"Yes," said Dr. Joe, firmly.

"But things are going so well here in Glasgow!" said Agnes.

"That is why we need to go to London; to teach this new antiseptic method to the doctors there. They are losing too many patients to infections."

"I see. It would be like it was here before young James came in with his broken leg," said Agnes.

"Yes, but we will not go alone, Agnes. I shall persuade some of our staff to come, so we will not have to start again from scratch."

"I shall start packing, dear Joseph," said Agnes.

"Agnes?"

"Yes?"

"While you're packing, pack for Europe, too. We've been invited to lecture on tour, so we'll do that before we settle in London."

"How exciting! At last doctors are beginning to heed your advice."

"Yes. Maybe now they will refrain from joking about microbes and take them seriously."

The day we walked into the main entrance of London's King's College Hospital, we became aware of the scorn.

"Here is the cat surgeon and he brought the cat to help him!"

Two of the interns began to laugh and a third added, "Shut the doors; you'll let in the microbes!"

Another one swatted the air saying, "They're invisible!"

But Dr. Joe was so cool. He nodded to the men as if they had paid him a compliment. He even said, "Good Morning!"

Then he and Agnes and I walked straight ahead to the administration office.

But just before the door closed, I heard one of the men say grimly, "Just wait until they meet the 'Head Cat.' She will take them down a peg or two!"

Meow! Were they mad at me, too? Who was the "Head Cat?" Why would she take us down a peg? It sounded grim, all right; but then the door closed and I couldn't hear any more of their jeers.

Inside, Dr. Joe spoke with the administrator and said, "I have brought my own staff and I can handle all the surgery for the ward. No other doctors will be needed."

The man blinked and sputtered a bit. "Never before … nursing supervisor … not going to like it …" and so on. Dr. Joe held his ground and ordered that his assigned ward be cleaned with his antiseptic solution. He supervised the cleaning of the operating room and set up his carbolic spraying machine. Agnes and his nurses worked hard to be sure all was the way it had been in Glasgow.

As they worked on the operating room, Dr. Joe and I went to the ward and there we met Sister Catherine, the Head Nurse. She was the nurse that the doctors called "Head Cat." The scowl on her face would have scared a barracuda.

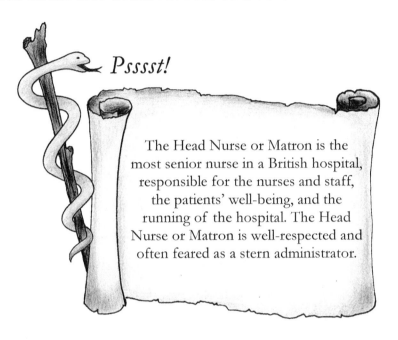

Pssst!

The Head Nurse or Matron is the most senior nurse in a British hospital, responsible for the nurses and staff, the patients' well-being, and the running of the hospital. The Head Nurse or Matron is well-respected and often feared as a stern administrator.

"No cats!" she scolded with a big huff and, scurrying over like a crab, gave me a kick from under her long skirts.

"No! Of course not!" said Dr. Joe. "Lexi, wait out in the corridor while I inspect the ward. Give yourself a bath."

As I collected my dignity and padded out to the hall, he smiled at "Sister Cat" and said most politely, "Please give me a tour of the ward and advise me of the condition of each patient."

"Yes, Dr. Lister. You can see my ward is in good order. I insist that the beds are made with precise corners and the linens are drawn tightly enough that you can bounce a coin on them.

It's the rotten smell of infection, all right!

I have been told that you insist on cleanliness. We make sure that the patients' faces are washed every day!"

I watched from the doorway as they approached the first bed. The patient's eyes were wide with fear.

My tail began to twitch!

"This patient has a broken leg," announced Sister Cat as she glared down at him.

Dr. Joe said, "So, you have broken your leg, Mr. ...?"

"Mr. Rafferty," whispered the man and looked at the head nurse as if he needed permission to speak.

Dr. Joe smiled, "Let's have a look, Mr. Rafferty." And he threw back the blanket and sheets.

The leg was set and held in place with splints. There was no open wound.

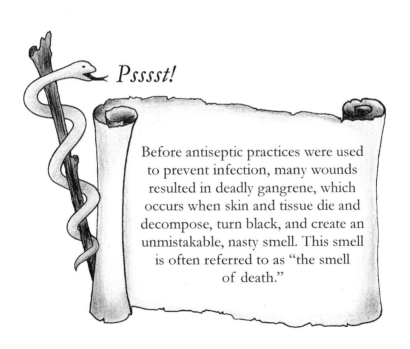

Psssst!

Before antiseptic practices were used to prevent infection, many wounds resulted in deadly gangrene, which occurs when skin and tissue die and decompose, turn black, and create an unmistakable, nasty smell. This smell is often referred to as "the smell of death."

Sister Cat said, "I could have told you, Doctor. You need not have destroyed the bed. From now on, leave the patients' care to me!"

"I'm sure you've done all you could, Sister, but from now on, I will be tending to the patients and changing their dressings myself. I have my own staff. There are new procedures that save lives and you may watch and learn if you wish."

Sister Cat's mouth set in a small tight line of disapproval. They continued along the row of beds. Some of the patients were asleep. My tail would not stop twitching ... and then I smelled it ... a terrible, rotten whiff of the dreaded ...

I followed my nose and ran across the ward to the last bed and began to claw frantically at the bed sheets, undoing the crisply folded "hospital corners." Dr. Joe turned and followed me rapidly. He threw back the sheets and called for Agnes and his nurses.

"Good for you, Lexi!" said Dr. Joe. "It's the rotten smell of infection all right. Hopefully, we can stop it in time, before it spreads, dear puss."

Sister Cat's face went purple with rage.

"You may have lectured all over Europe, but you are just a country doctor, and you will not rip apart my beds nor tell me my business!"

She huffed out of the ward and stamped on the tip of my tail as she stomped off.

"*Yeow!*" I screeched!

The patients applauded. "Yea! You told the tyrant!"

Dr. Joe was too busy washing the patient's wound with his antiseptic solution to pay them any attention.

Dr. Joe checked out the rest of the patients after he finished. He hadn't been assigned many patients, because the administrator didn't trust the new doctor either.

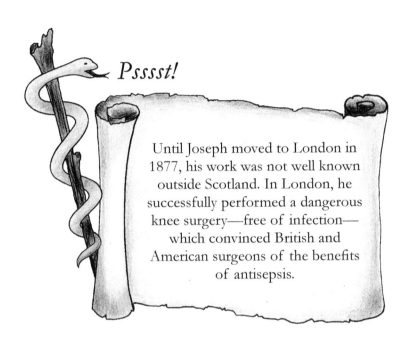

Psssst!

Until Joseph moved to London in 1877, his work was not well known outside Scotland. In London, he successfully performed a dangerous knee surgery—free of infection—which convinced British and American surgeons of the benefits of antisepsis.

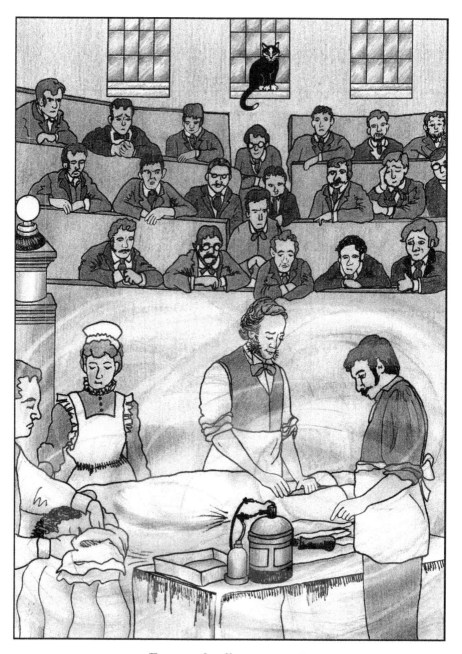

Doctors finally pay attention.

Chapter Eight

Defeat of Invisible Monsters

As a matter of fact, Dr. Joe had few patients until one day, a patient was referred to him by another doctor with the comment, "There is not much that can be done for him. He has a double compound fracture of his left leg and another compound fracture of his arm."

"What happened to him?" asked Dr. Joe.

"He fell off a building. There is not much hope. Do what you can. I will assist with the operation, but it looks hopeless."

Dr. Joe's eyes sparkled like a candlelit birthday cake. He and his staff set to work with great satisfaction. For the first time, a small audience of doctors watched from the gallery. When the operation was over, they silently left, shaking their heads in doubt.

For four days, all was quiet at the hospital. Then the news began to spread.

"There is no fever!" said one nurse to another. "I saw the wound and there is no pus either!"

"Truly?" said the second nurse. "You mean Dr. Lister can really defeat invisible monsters?"

"He can. He is amazing! This man fell off a roof and he will walk right out of the hospital. Dr. Lister says so."

"Those microbes have finally been defeated. Dr. Lister can do anything."

The doctors came to the ward to see for themselves. It was soon confirmed. The breaks had all been set and there was no gangrene.

I am a patient cat, but it wore my patience down, because it took such a long time before the doctors came to believe what they had seen with their own eyes. They held on to the theory that a chemical reaction to bad air caused flesh to rot. They could not accept that living but—practically speaking—"invisible" creatures in the air caused rot.

"How can a microbe so small we cannot see it cause such destruction in a creature as large as a human being?" asked one of the doctors.

"How can he claim that we doctors are contaminating our own patients? We are clean men; we do not work in the sewers. How dare he?" asked another.

And another said, "I followed most of his suggestions; I even used a ligature just once, and the wound still got infected!"

"And I tried his confounded carbolic acid! It burned my hands! They're still dry and cracked, and I'm still coughing, because it burned my lungs too!!" added a fourth.

But Dr. Joe would not give in to whining and complaints. He continued to instruct those who would listen. He also continued to improve his techniques.

Dr. Joe continued his experiments, and when he found that five percent carbolic acid solution killed bacteria, he diluted the solution so it wouldn't burn. He prepared it as a lotion to use on human skin. Dr. Joe also introduced the idea of steriliizing the tools and instruments used in surgery, rather than using strong solutions in sprays that irritated skin and lungs.

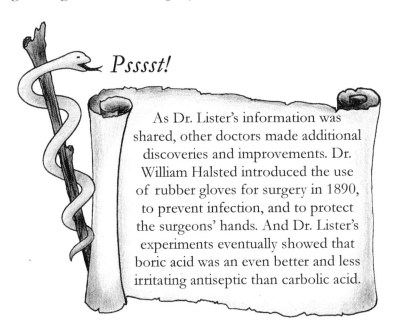

Pssst!

As Dr. Lister's information was shared, other doctors made additional discoveries and improvements. Dr. William Halsted introduced the use of rubber gloves for surgery in 1890, to prevent infection, and to protect the surgeons' hands. And Dr. Lister's experiments eventually showed that boric acid was an even better and less irritating antiseptic than carbolic acid.

And Dr. Joe paid particular attention to the threads called "ligatures" that doctors used to sew up a wound. He called the ligatures "catgut" and said the word repeatedly as he explained to Agnes different methods he could use to sterilize that "catgut."

I hissed at Dr. Joe every time he said "catgut." He tried to calm me down by petting me, so I leaped onto Agnes's lap and hissed and spat at him again.

Agnes laughed and said, "Dear Joe, please explain to Lexi that you don't mean HIS gut!"

"Oooooh!" said Dr. Joe. "No, Lexi, your guts are too small and delicate. We use sheep guts; they're much bigger and stronger. The same material is used as strings on a violin. A long time ago, fiddles or violins were called 'kits' so the material was called 'kit gut' and then it changed to 'catgut.'

"Don't worry, Lexi, catgut has nothing to do with you, dear puss!" And he scratched me behind my ear.

He and Agnes laughed again, and I was so relieved, I purred!

Dr. Joe did figure out how to sterilize the sheep gut and it was great, because it dissolved after time and he didn't have to operate again to remove the stitches.

Of course, more hopeless cases and other surgeries were referred to Dr. Joe. He even operated on a patient to remove a brain tumor.

His reputation in England was growing and he received an invitation to speak to the International Congress of Medical Science in Amsterdam. Dr. Joe practised his speech over and over to me. I was the only one who would listen after the fifteenth time. *Meow!*

I remember he made the point that medical doctors should pay attention to the information provided by the other branches of science. He had plenty of examples of the successes he'd experienced, because of the information he had received from Louis Pasteur and Tom Anderson.

I stayed home with Annie; I had heard the speech and my quiet, relaxed tail indicated that it would be a boring uneventful trip. However, the doctors in London began to use his methods and they didn't make fun of his microbes anymore. Finally, their mewing stopped.

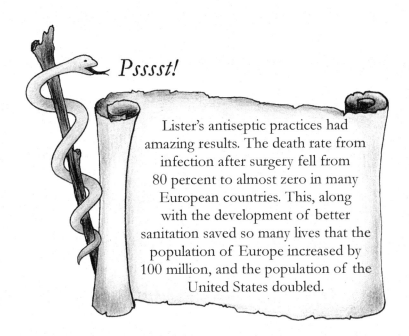

Pssst!

Lister's antiseptic practices had amazing results. The death rate from infection after surgery fell from 80 percent to almost zero in many European countries. This, along with the development of better sanitation saved so many lives that the population of Europe increased by 100 million, and the population of the United States doubled.

After his trip to Amsterdam, Dr. Joe was called in to the administration office where he was introduced to a Mr. Johnson, who was interested in Dr. Joe's bandaging techniques and design. He followed Dr. Joe to the hospital lab where Agnes was working and I was watching, and after several hours, Mr. Johnson left with notes and samples. Soon after, his company, Johnson & Johnson, produced bandaging called "Band-Aids" for the general public to use.

Pasteur identifies streptococcus.

CHAPTER NINE

A SURPRISE VISITOR

But it was Dr. Joe's next visitor who pleased him more than any other, and his arrival was a complete surprise. Agnes and Dr. Joe were working closely together in the lab as usual. They were completely absorbed in their project.

I was on the windowsill waiting to go home when there was a knock and a man entered and took off his top hat. "Pardon me. I hope I have the right room. I am looking for Joseph Lister. My name is Louis Pasteur."

"Mr. Pasteur! Yes, you have come to the right room. This is my wife, Agnes. It is such a tremendous pleasure to meet you!" said Dr. Joe.

"And I, you. I have heard great things about your work. You are saving so many lives."

"As many as I can," said Dr. Joe, modestly. "But none of it would have happened if it were not for your work."

"What are you working on today?" asked Louis. "May I look?"

"Of course!"

Louis looked into the microscope. "Ahh! Streptococcus! Now there is a nasty bacteria," said Louis. "I saw that microbe in 1869 and, believe it or not, later I was attending a lecture that featured that tiny monster and the lecturer said no one knew what it looked like, so I went up to the stage's blackboard and drew it for him. 'That is what it looks like!' I said."

Agnes and Dr. Joe laughed. I meowed. Agnes looked at me. "Oh, dear. I expect it is suppertime. Do come home with us for our evening meal, Louis. Annie is making us a pot roast."

"My favourite meal," said Louis with a smile.

After dinner that evening, Louis listened to the account of Bart's compound fracture and that of little Jimmy.

Dr. Joe said, "Following your good work, we knew we could not filter a body, nor heat it, so we looked for a chemical that would kill microbes and luckily we found one before those two accidents."

"In the field of observation, events favour only those who are prepared. And you certainly were," said Louis.

"Thanks to you, Louis."

"We must keep in touch, Joseph. We have much to share. I understand there is now an antiseptic solution named after you."

Dr. Joe laughed. "Yes. 'Listerine.' My staff say I could wash my mouth out with the product for saying some bad words."

"You never do that, Joseph!" said Agnes, staunchly defending him.

Dr. Joe laughed, "Well, now I have a mouthwash if I ever do. As much as 'Listerine' is a compliment, they have also named a nasty food bacteria after me, 'Listeria!' I cannot win!"

"I do wish to know of any of your new innovations in

medicine," said Louis. "Write to me as often as you can."

"Certainly," said Dr. Joe, "and I would be in your debt if you would keep me informed of any of your experiments and discoveries."

"*Certainement*," assured Louis.

After that, the mail service became extremely important. So I sat on the doorstep to be on the lookout for a letter from Louis Pasteur.

One day, a letter came. Louis wrote that the streptococcus bacteria had been visible in his microscope, and he was, therefore, able to devise an answer to the anthrax disease. But he could not see the microbe that caused rabies, because it was too small.

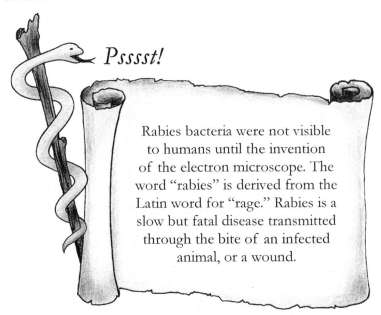

Pssst!

Rabies bacteria were not visible to humans until the invention of the electron microscope. The word "rabies" is derived from the Latin word for "rage." Rabies is a slow but fatal disease transmitted through the bite of an infected animal, or a wound.

Louis continued, "Because I cannot see it, I must logically reason that, as rabies is spread through a bite or a wound, it must be in the saliva. The disease affects the brain and spinal cord, so if I can isolate it from those sources, perhaps I can obtain enough to create a vaccine.

Dr. Joe and Agnes wrote back to encourage Louis's work.

Pasteur's trials and experiments investigating the horrible disease of rabies took three years. Meanwhile, I stayed away from any angry animals that might give me the disease!

At last, Louis obtained infected tissue from a rabbit. He put it into a solution and he worked to weaken the solution until he could use it as a vaccine.

We waited for weeks for his next letter. Finally, a letter arrived, and Agnes eagerly opened it. In it, Pasteur announced that the long process of injections actually worked on dogs, both as a treatment and as a preventative vaccine.

Soon after, Dr. Joe was very excited by another letter from Louis.

"Agnes! Louis has saved a nine-year-old boy who was bitten fourteen times by a rabid dog. It took weeks of injections, but the boy survived! We are so lucky to have Pasteur in this world!"

We then heard in the news stories of Pasteur saving many lives from rabies. He was now world famous!

Dr. Joe was becoming more famous himself. In honour of his life-saving work, Dr. Joe was knighted by Queen Victoria in 1883. Then, four years later, Dr. Joe was further honoured as a Baron, and was now referred to as Lord Lister.

Psssst!

The nine-year-old boy, Joseph Meister, did not develop rabies, even though he'd been bitten by the rabid dog so many times, and when he grew up, he became the doorman for the Pasteur Institute.

In the fall of 1892, Dr. Joe and Agnes received an invitation to celebrate Louis Pasteur's seventieth birthday at the Sorbonne in Paris. Agnes carried me in her carpetbag, as usual. When we arrived in Paris, it seemed like the whole city was ready to celebrate, with street posters and souvenirs. The doorman at the Sorbonne looked a little critically at the size of Agnes's "purse," but she just smiled at him and he never suspected there was a puss in her purse. The ushers gave everyone a portrait medal of Pasteur.

The great auditorium was packed with professors and scientists from many countries. We were ushered into seats close to the front, and saw Louis escorted into the seat of honour by the President of France.

As the room applauded Louis Pasteur's entrance, Agnes whispered, "Louis has aged, dear Joseph. He is apparently still suffering from the stroke he had twenty years ago."

Happy Birthday, Louis!

"Yes," Dr. Joe agreed, "but he is still working, in spite of that."

There were many speeches of congratulations. Dr. Joe greeted Louis in person with his good wishes too, and then we waited for Louis's own speech. His words spoke of his years of work and his belief that "science and peace will triumph over ignorance and war ... the future will belong not to the conquerors, but to those who have done the most for suffering humanity," and Louis looked at Dr. Joe.

Dr. Joe and Louis kept up their friendship as long as they lived.

Several years later, in 1897, I travelled with Dr. Joe to Canada, to attend a medical meeting in Montreal. We then travelled west to Vancouver Island, British Columbia. Dr. John Chapman Davie met us in Victoria and we rode in a horse-drawn carriage to the Royal Jubilee Hospital to see its new operating room.

Dr. Davie proudly led the tour of the new operating facility that he had designed according to Dr. Joe's principles of antisepsis. It had a beautiful tiled floor, so cool on my paws. But the best part was the circle of windows around the octagonal room. I leaped up onto each and every sill as Dr. Joe inspected the room. The light was good from every angle and I could watch everyone. *Yeow!* I was having a great time until Dr. Davie noticed me and shooed me out.

Royal Jubilee Hospital's Pemberton Operating Room, Victoria, Canada

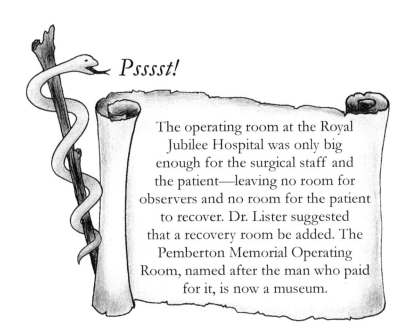

Psssst!

The operating room at the Royal Jubilee Hospital was only big enough for the surgical staff and the patient—leaving no room for observers and no room for the patient to recover. Dr. Lister suggested that a recovery room be added. The Pemberton Memorial Operating Room, named after the man who paid for it, is now a museum.

"No cats allowed in my operating room!"

Dr. Joe and I exchanged a look. We both remembered the "Head Cat" kicking me off the ward. Dr. Joe laughed. I scurried out to the hallway, avoiding a possible kick from Dr. Davie. After all, he didn't wear a long skirt to muffle the kick!

I gave myself a bath to restore my dignity.

I am only a cat, but I'm proud of it! *Meow!*

And I must add, that Lord Joseph Lister was a cool cat; today, he is referred to as "The Father of Modern Surgery."

Meow!

PAWSCRIPT

Thousands of years ago, cats were worshipped as gods.
Cats have never forgotten this.
~ Anonymous

GLOSSARY

Amputate:
To amputate is to surgically remove a part of the body.

Anesthetic:
An anesthetic is a substance, like a medicine, that takes away the feeling of pain. It is often used before surgery.

Antisepsis/Antiseptic:
Antisepsis means the destruction of harmful microorganisms. Something is called "antiseptic" if it kills harmful bacteria.

Bacteria:
Bacteria are one-celled organisms (microbes) living everywhere, such as in the soil, the air, in dust or in or on the body. The word comes from the Greek word for "little stick."

Boric acid:
Boric acid is made from borax, a mineral salt. It is used as a mild antiseptic and household cleaner.

Carbolic acid or phenol:
Carbolic acid is also known as phenol. It used to be made from coal tar, and is now made from petroleum. It is a disinfectant.

Carpetbag:
A carpetbag is a travelling bag or carryall, made of a carpet-like material. It was popular in the nineteenth century.

Compound fracture:

A compound fracture is an injury in which a piece of bone has broken through the skin, causing a greater risk of infection.

Creosote:

Creosote is a colourless, oily liquid distilled from wood tar and used as an antiseptic.

Gangrene:

Gangrene is the decomposition and death of soft body tissue, usually caused by infection or from blocked circulation. Treatment can include amputation.

Immunity/Immunology:

Immunity is the ability of an organism to resist or fight off an infection. The branch of science that studies the immune system is called "Immunology."

Infection:

An infection is a harmful condition caused by the invasion of the body by bacteria, viruses, or fungi.

The Lancet:

The Lancet is a world-famous, British medical journal, established in 1823. It is the longest-running medical journal in the world, and is an important way for doctors to communicate their discoveries. It was named after a small two-edged surgical knife with a sharp point.

Ligature:
A ligature is something used in surgery to tie off a blood vessel, often thread-like. Ligatures are sometimes called sutures.

Laudanum:
Laudanum is a medicine that was used as a painkiller and sedative in the nineteenth century.

Listeria:
Named after Dr. Lister, Listeria is a bacteria that can infect food, especially delicatessen meats and dairy products.

Miasma:
Miasma—or "bad air"—is from the Greek word for "pollution." It is often bad smelling, usually from rotting material. Before the medical community accepted the germ theory, they believed that diseases were caused by miasma.

Microbe:
Microbes are living organisms too small to be seen without a microscope. They include bacteria, viruses, and fungi. The word comes from the Greek words for "small" (mikros) and "life" (bios).

Obstetrics:
Obstetrics is the branch of medicine that specializes in childbirth, and caring for women before, during, and after childbirth.

Puerperal Fever:

Also known as childbed fever, puerperal fever is a life-threatening infection of women's reproductive organs, contaminated at the time of birth or miscarriage.

Puke:

"Puke" and "puking" are other words for "vomit" and "vomiting."

Sepsis:

Sepsis can be a life-threatening complication from an infection.

Surgery:

Surgery is the name of medical treatments where a doctor cuts into a body to repair, remove, or replace parts that are damaged or diseased.

Streptococcus:

Streptococcus is a kind of bacteria. Various species of streptococcus can cause diseases such as pneumonia, "strep" throat, and scarlet fever. Other species are used in the food industry to make butter and cheese.

Virus:

A virus is a submicroscopic organism that invades and multiplies inside the living cells of plants and animals, causing an infection.

IMPORTANT DATES

1546

Girolamo Fracastoro, an Italian physician, suggests that tiny particles like "seeds" or "spores" cause epidemics, and that they can travel long distances.

1795

Alexander Gordon, a Scottish physician publishes a paper suggesting that doctors and nurses spread puerperal or childbed fever.

1796

Edward Jenner, an English physician and scientist, pioneers the world's first vaccine, the smallpox vaccine.

1822

Louis Pasteur is born December 27, 1822.

1827

Joseph Lister is born April 5, 1827.

1830

Joseph Jackson Lister (Joseph Lister's father) improves the microscope.

1843

Oliver Wendell Holmes, an American physician, publishes *The Contagiousness of Puerperal Fever*, claiming that puerperal fever was spread by doctors and nurses.

1852

Joseph graduates from medical school with high honours at age 25.

1855

Joseph Lister starts his fellowship in Edinburgh under Scottish surgeon James Syme.

1856

Joseph marries Agnes Syme, daughter of James Syme. Joseph becomes an assistant surgeon and lecturer at age 29.

1859

Joseph becomes Professor of Medicine at Glasgow University.

1860

Joseph becomes Professor of Surgery at Glasgow University.

1865

Thomas Anderson, a Scottish chemist, informs Joseph about French chemist and microbiologist Louis Pasteur's work with microbes.

Joseph begins to use carbolic acid in surgery to prevent infection. He operates on an eleven-year-old boy with a compound fracture.

1867

Joseph publishes a series of articles in *The Lancet*.

1871
Joseph successfully treats Queen Victoria for an abscess in Glasgow.

1875
Joseph lectures on antiseptic practices in Germany and France.

1876
Joseph travels to America and speaks about his success with antiseptic techniques. Robert Wood Johnson hears him speak, and is inspired to start a company with his brothers (Johnson & Johnson) to mass produce sterile surgical dressings and sutures according to Lister's methods. The Johnson brothers launched their company in 1886.

1879
"Listerine" is invented by two Americans as a surgical antiseptic, and named after Joseph Lister. It was shared with dentists for oral care in 1895, and became popular as an over-the-counter mouthwash in 1915.

1880
Joseph and Agnes move to London, England.

1881
Louis Pasteur travels to London and visits Joseph.

1882
Louis Pasteur studies rabies, and creates a vaccine in 1885.

1883

Joseph is knighted by Queen Victoria. He is now referred to as Sir Lister.

1886

Joseph introduces the practice of sterilizing surgical instruments using steam.

1887

Joseph is further honoured by Queen Victoria and made a Baron. He is now referred to as Lord Lister.

1890

William Halsted, American physician and surgeon, introduces the use of rubber gloves during surgery to prevent infection and protect surgeons' and nurses' hands.

1892

Joseph and Agnes attend Louis Pasteur's seventieth birthday party at the Sorbonne.

1893

Agnes dies of pneumonia. Joseph retires.

1895

Louis Pasteur dies.

1896

The Pemberton Operating Room at the Royal Jubilee Hospital in Victoria, Canada opens. In 1995, the Pemberton Memorial Operating Room is designated a National Historic Site.

1897

Joseph visits the Royal Jubilee Hospital's Pemberton Operating Room. He suggests that a recovery room be added.

1912

Joseph dies on February 10, 1912, at his country home in Kent, at age eighty-four.

IMPORTANT PEOPLE

Almost all the characters in this story are true, as are their accomplishments. The only characters created for the story are Dorie, Annie, and Sister Catherine, the Head Nurse.

Thomas Anderson was a Scottish chemist who made many contributions to organic and agricultural chemistry. He advised his friend and colleague Joseph Lister on Louis Pasteur's germ theory and suggested the use of carbolic acid as an antiseptic.

John Chapman Davie Jr. was a Canadian physician and surgeon, who studied under Joseph Lister during a European sabbatical. He was the chief medical officer at the Royal Jubilee Hospital in Victoria, Canada. When the hospital received a bequest from Joseph Pemberton and his family, Davie campaigned for an operating room that used Joseph Lister's principles of antisepsis. The Pemberton Operating Room was opened in 1896 and Joseph Lister visited the operating room in 1897.

Girolamo Fracastoro was an Italian physician, poet, mathematician, and scholar who, in 1546, suggested that tiny particles caused epidemics, and that these seed-like particles could travel from person to person or through the air. He suggested that clothes and linens could hold onto these particles, further spreading disease. His theories could not be proven until the invention and further development of microscopes.

Alexander Gordon was a Scottish obstetrician and naval surgeon. In 1795 he published a paper that warned that puerperal or childbed fever was spread by doctors and nurses. He recommended that doctors and nurses wash themselves and their clothes, that rooms be cleaned, and that linens of infected mothers be burned. His paper was not well received by his colleagues.

Oliver Wendell Holmes was an American physician, professor, poet, and essayist. In 1843 he published an article, *The Contagiousness of Puerperal Fever*, in which he argued the fever was spread by the attending doctors and nurses. He further suggested that a physician with a patient with puerperal or childbed fever should purify his instruments, burn the clothing worn attending that patient, and not practise obstetrics for at least six months. His paper was not well received by his colleagues.

Edward Jenner was an English scientist and country doctor at a time when smallpox was killing many people. He listened to the local folklore that milkmaids never got smallpox, and noticed that his milkmaid patients got blisters or pocks on their hands from milking cows infected with cowpox. In 1796, he applied some pus from a milkmaid's blister onto a scratch on an eight-year-old boy's arm, and later exposed the boy to smallpox. The boy was immune. He repeated the procedure. He called the substance "a vaccine," from the Latin word "vacca" meaning "cow." Jenner's work is said to have "saved more lives than the work of any other human," and he is referred to as the Father of Immunology.

Robert Wood Johnson was an American businessman who was inspired by a speech Joseph Lister gave in America about antiseptic practices in surgery. Robert founded the company Johnson & Johnson with his brothers, and they mass-produced sterile bandages, sutures, and surgical supplies.

Agnes Syme Lister was the daughter of Scottish surgeon James Syme, and the wife of Joseph Lister. On their honeymoon, Agnes and Joseph toured many hospitals and universities in France and Germany. Agnes became interested in medical research and became Joseph's laboratory partner.

Joseph Jackson Lister was a wealthy British wine merchant who was fascinated with microscopes as a hobby. He invented the achromatic or compound microscope, which eliminated the rainbow effect that distorted images. For this, he was elected as a Fellow of the Royal Society of London for Improving Natural Knowledge. He was the father of Joseph Lister.

Joseph Lister was a British surgeon who pioneered antiseptic surgery. As a boy he drew plants and animals, including a frog skeleton that looked ready to leap. He started college at the University College of London at age sixteen, and decided to study medicine at seventeen. He studied anatomy, the arts, and both French and German. After graduation he was advised by one of his teachers to study with James Syme, Professor of Surgery, in Scotland. Joseph went to Scotland, studied with Syme, became his assistant, and married his daughter Agnes.

Joseph's success with antiseptics allowed him to be more inventive with the art of surgery, and he made many improvements in medicine. He used rubber tubing to drain pus from abscesses; he joined broken bones with silver wire; and from an experiment on a calf, he discovered that ligatures made from sheep intestines dissolved in a few weeks and did not need to be removed. He also improved the surgical technique for mastectomies, and developed a method of repairing kneecaps with metal wire.

In recognition of his important work, Joseph received awards and honours throughout his lifetime.

Louis Pasteur was a French chemist and bacteriologist who showed that living microorganisms caused fermentation. He showed that microbes could decompose wine, resulting in vinegar, and microbes caused milk to become sour. He proved that if bacteria-free fluids were heated, then the fluids could remain free of bacteria. This work resulted in the process of pasteurization, named after him. Pasteur also worked to isolate the bacteria causing anthrax and chicken cholera, and made vaccines against them. He pioneered vaccinations against rabies, and investigated the disease of silkworms, saving the silk industry.

Ignaz Philip Semmelweis was an Austro-Hungarian obstetrician who discovered the infectious character of puerperal fever, also known as childbed fever. He demonstrated that handwashing could reduce the number of deaths after childbirth. He was the Director of the maternity clinic at the

Vienna General Hospital in the 1840s, and kept statistics until he was convinced that infection was spread by the hands of doctors, especially those who did autopsies and then treated maternity patients. He advocated rigorous cleanliness and handwashing in his obstetrical clinics. He published a book outlining his findings, but as they conflicted with the practices of the times, the medical and scientific community rejected them. Not until Louis Pasteur proved the germ theory and Joseph Lister proved the success of antiseptic methods did the medical community implement practices of cleanliness. Semmelweis has been called the "saviour of the mothers."

James Syme was a Scottish physician and surgeon, with a strong interest in chemistry. Joseph Lister became James's assistant at the University of Edinburgh and at the Edinburgh Royal Infirmary, and he married James's daughter Agnes in 1856.

AUTHOR'S NOTE TO PARENTS AND TEACHERS

Dear Parents and Teachers,

I have been asked why I have written so many stories about history as seen through the eyes of a cat. I have two reasons.

First, I am fulfilling the universal human wish to be a fly on the wall or an invisible witness. My cat is the proverbial fly on the wall, because a cat has an amazing ability to stay incredibly still and blend into its surroundings. A cat can also hide in unexpected places.

Second, children need to have heroes to admire and to inspire them. I have chosen to depict heroes from real life who are worthy of their attention. History is amazing. It relates to us the deeds and misdeeds of people. It then exposes the thinking that caused those good and bad actions by the visual means of arts and by written records.

No lesson from history is more amazing than the examples of man's creativity. For example, creative thinking brought about the pyramids and the harnessing of atomic energy.

In the series *Lexi Catt's Meowmoirs—Tales of Heroic Scientists*, I have focused on mankind's creative developments in the field of human health sciences. Though subjected to superstitions, religious taboos, political expediency, and financial greed, the development of mankind's understanding and preservation of human health is awe-inspiring. I salute the heroes who have courageously brought new insights to us, such as Imhotep, Hippocrates, Marie Curie, Leonardo da Vinci, Joseph Lister, and Linus Pauling.

Perhaps you, too, and your children, will be amazed and in-spired as we look at these heroes and their adventures through the eyes of a cat known as Lexi, Alexander Catt II.

Cheers,

Marian Keen

P.S. I thought you might like to know some of the piquant tidbits in the following pages, which my research uncovered; they are interesting but not necessary to the story.

WHY DID LISTER SUCCEED WHERE OTHERS HAD FAILED?

Joseph Lister valued the many contributions made from other branches of science, such as those made by Louis Pasteur and Thomas Anderson. Lister also used the microscope, performed his own experiments, kept records, published his results, taught his procedures to others, and invented new applications. He used antiseptics to clean the operating room, the instruments, the bandaging, and the air, inventing a machine to do so.

Others blamed sepsis or infection on bad air, the weather, the patient, polar air currents, etc. They refused to believe there were microbes involved, because they couldn't be seen with the naked eye. They believed that antiseptics had been used before without effect, so they decided not to bother, and they often didn't follow directions.

In the 1800s, it was considered a professional courtesy to allow others to view an operation, wearing their street clothes. These guests shook hands with the surgeon and remained close to the operation. Dropped instruments were retrieved and handed back to the surgeon. The surgeons and assistants did not cover their faces, hair, or hands (surgical gloves were not invented until 1895). Surgeons used handkerchiefs to wipe sweat, blow their noses, and clean spectacles, and then continued the operation.

It has always been difficult to fight invisible microbes. In today's world, the concern is with super-resistant bacteria. In the nineteenth century, much concern centred on puerperal fever, which killed women by the thousands. While conventional thinking was in denial, some doctors were slowly realizing the truth, that the fever was contagious and that medical staff played a role in passing on the germs. Some of these doctors included Ignaz Semmelweis, Alexander Gordon, and Oliver Wendell Holmes.

The Microscope
Key to the Success of Lister and Pasteur

The scientific progress made by Joseph Lister and Louis Pasteur would not have been possible without the invention of and improvements made to the microscope by optometrists, naturalists, merchants, mathematicians, and engineers. Here is a short history of the microscope's development.

In the fourteenth century, the grinding of lenses to improve eyesight began in Italy.

In Holland in 1595, the first compound microscope was made by Zacharias Janssen. He was ten years old at the time. It was a simple tube with lenses on each end. It magnified the image by between three and nine times.

Soon after, the Dutch scientist Anton van Leeuwenhoek made a simple microscope with one lens, but the lens was so good that he was the first person to describe bacteria. He also observed protozoa (tiny organisms) in a drop of pond water.

At the same time, British natural philosopher Robert Hooke confirmed Leeuwenhoek's observations, and used the word "cell" to describe microscopic structures.

In 1830, Joseph Jackson Lister improved the compound lens system by spacing out larger lenses to correct flaws, such as a lack of focus and definition. Lister also eliminated the distracting rainbow effects and coloured outlines to define images more clearly. Lister was the first to see human blood cells, and he trained his son, Joseph Lister, in the use of the microscope.

In the early twentieth century, microscopes advanced further, to allow the study of objects below the wavelength of light, and to allow the study of transparent biological materials.

Then in 1938, Ernst Ruska, a German engineering student, and his mentor Max Knoll developed the electron microscope. This greatly improved the visibility of the smallest detail, and finally made viruses visible.

Up to this time, scientists could only deduce the existence of viruses, which were too small to be seen or filtered. With the use of the electron microscope, scientists discovered that these tiny viruses existed in a great range of sizes. Scientists were also now able to see the differences between the smallpox virus and the chickenpox virus. The polio virus was first seen in 1952. Since the 1950s, many other viruses have been identified and classified.

WHERE ARE MICROBES?

Microbes—a group that includes bacteria, fungi, and viruses—are everywhere, from above the clouds to miles below ground. They travel in the air we breathe that carries dust, pollen, sea spray, volcanic ash, and plant spores. Some microbes cause improved health; some cause illness.

There are trillions of good bacteria in each human body, which is a good thing, because they prevent tooth decay, kill pathogens, inhibit harmful bacteria, aid digestion, help to absorb nutrients, regulate body weight, build immunity, and ward off autoimmune diseases.

Bacteria-infecting viruses called bacteriophages or "phages" for short, are the most abundant life form on Earth, exceeding the number of stars. Microbes even reproduce in clouds, and ice crystals are able to form around them creating snowflakes.

No wonder moms tell their children not to eat snow!

PASTEUR—A GENEROUS GENIUS

As a professor of chemistry and head of the science faculty at the University of Lille in France, Louis Pasteur was asked to investigate various problems of the industrial world. Pasteur generously shared all his knowledge with other scientists for the benefit of mankind.

He discovered that microbes were the cause of many issues, such as putrefaction (the rotting of meat); fermentation (the breakdown of sugars) of fruit juices into wine; and infections of silk worms in the silk industry. He could see the microbes in his microscope.

He investigated the process of fermentation, and invented pasteurization (treating with heat) of wine and milk. Pasteurization prevented wine from turning into vinegar, and milk from souring.

Knowing that microbes or "germs" could cause problems in animals, Louis Pasteur treated children with cholera, and cows and sheep with anthrax via vaccination, as Edward Jenner had done with smallpox. Pasteur then found that the insertion of a few of the microbes of a disease into a host could allow the person or animal to build immunity against that disease.

He next investigated rabies, which has been called the "world's oldest infectious disease," and is almost always fatal. The symptoms of rabies show that it attacks the spinal cord and brain, and seems to spread through a bite or wound. However, no bacteria or microbe was visible through the microscope, so Pasteur had to work by deduction and theory. Rabies (from the Latin word for "rage") took anywhere from ten days to two months from the time of the bite or exposure to the infection until symptoms developed. Pasteur used the infected spinal cord tissue from rabbits to create a vaccine. He administered this vaccine gradually, every day, for two weeks to dogs to prevent or cure the rabies. His careful work on animals took three years.

In July 1885, a nine-year-old boy, Joseph Meister, was bitten multiple times by a rabid dog. His mother begged Pasteur to use his new vaccine on her son. After two weeks of vaccine injections, the boy survived, and developed no symptoms of rabies.

Pasteur became world-famous for developing a cure for rabies. In December 1885, four boys from New Jersey, USA, who had been bitten by a rabid dog, were sent to Pasteur in France for the same successful cure. And in 1886, nineteen Russian peasants from Smolensk who had been bitten by a rabid wolf were sent to Pasteur for treatment. Sixteen of them survived. The Czar rewarded Pasteur with money, which was used to establish an institute for the treatment of rabies. In due time, the Pasteur Institute was built in Paris, and Joseph Meister was hired as the institute's doorman.

HOW TO AVOID NASTY MICROBES—
THE ONES THAT MAKE US SICK

More than one hundred years ago, scientists, doctors, and nurses learned that microbes cause infections and illnesses. They also learned that proper sanitation saves people's lives and limbs from infection. Yet today, we all still need to be reminded to wash our hands.

The United Nations declared 2008 as the International Year of Sanitation, and Global Handwashing Day was launched. It takes place every year on October 15, and millions of people in over a hundred countries participate. Washing hands routinely could save more lives than any single vaccine or medical discovery.

Yet in 2009, surveys showed that some medical staff were still not washing their hands enough. Campaigns continued to demand handwashing in hospitals, and hand sanitizers were placed around conveniently to encourage compliance. It is recommended that alcohol-based sanitizers are reliable and have no side effects or toxins when used properly.

Keeping in mind that hands are the basic means of passing along infections, wash your hands:

- after sneezing
- before and after eating
- after using the toilet
- after wiping your nose.

Use lots of soap and water, and wash your hands for at least as long as takes you to sing the happy birthday song to yourself. If soap and water are not available, then use an alcohol-based gel sanitizer. And keep your hands off your face!

BIBLIOGRAPHY

Glasscheib, H.S., MD. *The March of Medicine the Emergence and Triumph of Modern Medicine.* New York: G.P. Putman's Sons, NY., and Toronto: Longmans Canada, Ltd., 1963.

Hird, Ed., Reverend, Dr. "Dr. Joseph Lister: Medical Revolutionary." *Deep Cove Crier.* January 1988.

Humphreys, Danda, RN. "Past progressive: Historic Operating Room a Monument to the Advent of Antisepsis." *Canadian Medical Association Journal*, 178, No. 2. January 15, 2008. Pages 193-194.

Margotta, Roberto. *History of Medicine.* Diane Publishing Co. 2001.

McTavish, Douglas. *Joseph Lister, Pioneers of Science.* East Sussex, England: Wayland Publishers, Ltd., 1991.

Nuland, Sherwin B. *The Doctors' Plague: Germs, Childbed Fever, and the Strange Story of Ignac Semmelweis (Great Discoveries).* New York: Atlas Books, W.W. Norton & Co., 2003.

Porter, Roy, MD. *Medicine—A History of Healing: Ancient Traditions to Modern Practices.* New York: Marlowe & Co., 1997.

Strathern, Paul. *A Brief History of Medicine: From Hippocrates' Four Humours to Crick and Watson's Double Helix (Brief History Series)*. London, England: Constable & Robinson, 2005.

Tuchman, Barbara. *The Proud Tower: A Portrait of the World Before the War, 1890-1914*. Bantam Books, 1996.

Wolfe, Nathan. "The Secret World of Microbes." *National Geographic*. January, 2013. Pages 136-147.

Wikipedia, "Global Handwashing Day."

Wikipedia, "Joseph Lister."

Marian Keen, B.S. in Education, Central Connecticut State University, has been writing in a variety of genres since the early 1980s. Marian majored in middle-grade education, and taught grades five and six.

In *Lexi Catt's Meowmoirs—Tales of Heroic Scientists*, the talented feline Lexi shares his adventures with heroes who have made discoveries in the fields of science and medicine, including Joseph Lister, the Father of Modern Surgery.

Marian's works and commentary can be found at: megsbooks.com and stresstonics.com.

ABOUT THE AUTHOR

Marian Keen has been writing in a variety of genres since the 1980s, with a special interest in historical fiction for children and youth.

Marian's middle-grade stories for children include the *Adventures of Alexander Catt*, and *Lexi Catt's Meowmoirs—Tales of Heroic Scientists*. These "meowmoirs" bring to life famous people and significant milestones in science, medicine, art, exploration, and human development:

- *Lexi & Hippocrates Find Trouble at the Olympics*
- *Lexi & Marie Curie Saving Lives in World War I*
- *Lexi & Lister Defeat Death*

Look for new titles to be released soon.

Her stories for young readers feature British Columbian animals such as skunks, racoons, owls, bears, squirrels, crows, and seagulls. A complete list of works, including her poetry, can be found at megsbooks.com.

Verity, also published by Influence Publishing, is her first published novel for teens.

With a life-long interest in nutrition, healthy living, and illness prevention, Marian's health articles can be found at: stresstonics.com.

Jodie Dias, BA, Art History, University of British Columbia, is a children's illustrator, painter, designer, and photographer. Her whimsical style brings life to *Lexi Catt's Meowmoirs—Tales of Heroic Scientists*. Her previous works include *Lexi and Hippocrates Find Trouble at the Olympics*; *Lexi and Marie Curie Saving Lives in WWI*; *Abigail Skunk's Lessons for Her Kits*; and *Alexander Catt's Kitty Letters for Kids* In the Lexi Series, Jodie's playful imagery is set in historically accurate settings.

She was production manager for the children's animated movie, *Legend of the Candy Cane*; partner and graphic designer with Keen Designs; and a commissioned portrait artist.

Wendy Watson, BFA, University of Victoria, is a visual artist, designer, wood-block print maker, watercolour painter, and professional photographer with superb production and finishing techniques. Her children's illustrative works include *Lexi and Hippocrates Find Trouble at the Olympics*; *Lexi and Marie Curie Saving Lives in WWI*; and *Abigail Skunk's Lessons for Her Kits*.

Her works have been shown in many Vancouver-area galleries; she was a partner and designer with Keen Designs; she is a commissioned artist; and she currently works at Langara College.

If you want to get on the path to becoming a published author with Influence Publishing please go to www.InfluencePublishing.com

Inspiring books that influence change

More information on our other titles and how to submit your own proposal can be found at www.InfluencePublishing.com

CPSIA information can be obtained at www.ICGtesting.com
Printed in the USA
LVOW04s2035150315

430606LV00009B/53/P

9 781771 410977